A first guide to

◆

Ireland

By Kath Davies

A ZOË BOOK

A ZOË BOOK

© 1997 Zoë Books Limited

Devised and produced by
Zoë Books Limited
15 Worthy Lane
Winchester
Hampshire SO23 7AB
England

COUNTRIES
MBN-C
)1-97
ASK

First published in Great Britain in 1997 by
Zoë Books Limited
15 Worthy Lane
Winchester
Hampshire SO23 7AB

A record of the CIP data is available from the British Library.

ISBN 1 874488 95 9

Printed in Italy by Grafedit SpA
Editor: Manda Joyce
Design and Production: Sterling Associates
Map: Gecko Limited

Photographic acknowledgments

The publishers wish to acknowledge, with thanks, the following photographic sources:

Cover and title page: Impact/Geray Sweeney; 5l Impact/Michael Dent; 5r Zefa; 6 Impact/Michael George; 7l Robert Harding Picture Library/Dominic Harcourt-Webster; 7r Impact/Brian Harris; 8 Robert Harding Picture Library/Roy Rainford; 9l Impact/Paul O'Driscoll; 9r Impact/Bob Hobby; 10, 11l Robert Harding Picture Library/Philip Craven; 11r Allsport/Mike Hewitt; 12 Impact/Bruce Stephens; 13l Robert Harding Picture Library/Duncan Maxwell; 13r Impact/Michael Dent; 14,15l&r,16 Impact/Geray Sweeney; 17l Impact/Michael Dent; 17r Impact/Geray Sweeney; 18 Robert Harding Picture Library/RogerStowell; 19l Impact/David Reed; 19r Impact/Geray Sweeney; 20 Impact/Paul O'Driscoll; 21l&r Sporting Pictures (UK); 22 Robert Harding Picture Library/Dominic Harcourt-Webster; 23l *William Butler Yeats* by Augustus John (1878-1961) Manchester City Art Galleries/Bridgeman Art Library; 23r,24, 25l&r Ancient Art & Architecture Collection; 26 Philip Sauvain Picture Collection; 27l Mary Evans Picture Library; 27r Philip Sauvain Picture Collection; 28 The Mansell Collection; 29l Impact/John Arthur; 29r Impact/Geray Sweeney

The publishers have made every effort to trace the copyright holders, but if they have inadvertently overlooked any, they will be pleased to make the necessary arrangement at the first opportunity.

Cover: *Horse riding on the beach, County Sligo*

Title page: *The Giant's Causeway, County Antrim*

Contents

Irish words are shown in *italics* and are explained in the text.

4

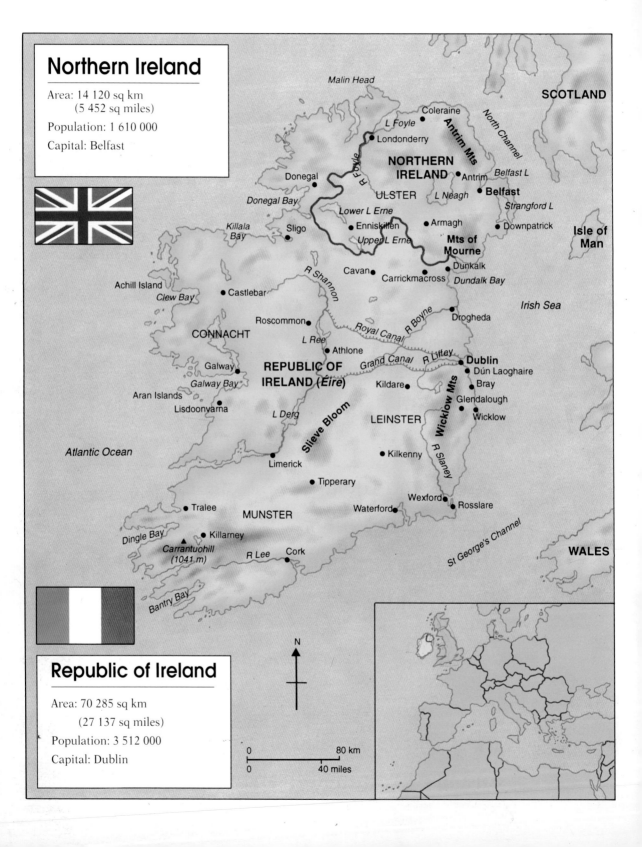

Northern Ireland

Area: 14 120 sq km
(5 452 sq miles)

Population: 1 610 000

Capital: Belfast

Republic of Ireland

Area: 70 285 sq km
(27 137 sq miles)

Population: 3 512 000

Capital: Dublin

Malin Head

SCOTLAND

Coleraine

L Foyle

Londonderry

Antrim Mts

North Channel

NORTHERN
IRELAND

Antrim

Belfast L

Donegal

Belfast

Donegal Bay

ULSTER

L Neagh

Strangford L

Lower L Erne

Armagh

Downpatrick

Isle of
Man

Killala
Bay

Sligo

Enniskillen

Upper L Erne

Mts of
Mourne

R Shannon

Cavan

Carrickmacross

Dunkalk

Dundalk Bay

Achill Island

Clew Bay

Castlebar

Irish Sea

Roscommon

Royal Canal

R Boyne

Drogheda

CONNACHT

L Ree

Athlone

Grand Canal

R Liffey

Dublin

Galway

REPUBLIC OF
IRELAND (Éire)

Dún Laoghaire

Galway Bay

Kildare

Bray

Aran Islands

Glendalough

Lisdoonvarna

L Derg

Wicklow Mts

Wicklow

Atlantic Ocean

Slieve Bloom

LEINSTER

R Slaney

Limerick

Kilkenny

Tipperary

Tralee

MUNSTER

Wexford

Rosslare

Waterford

Dingle Bay

Killarney

St George's Channel

WALES

Carrantuohill
(1041 m)

R Lee

Cork

Bantry Bay

N

0   80 km

0   40 miles

Céad Míle Fáilte!

"A hundred thousand welcomes!"

Ireland is an island on the northwestern edge of Europe.

To the west, Ireland faces the stormy Atlantic Ocean. The seas have worn away bays and inlets. To the east, the Irish Sea lies between Ireland and Great Britain.

The centre of Ireland is farmland. There are hills and low mountains around this central plain.

▲ A farm in the countryside

▼ A post office in the Irish Republic

Ireland's climate is mild and damp. The green fields have given the country its nickname, 'The Emerald Isle'.

Ireland has four parts, or provinces, Leinster, Munster, Ulster and Connacht. They are divided into 32 counties.

Six counties in Ulster make up Northern Ireland, part of the United Kingdom. All the other counties form the Republic of Ireland, which is a separate country.

Irish is one of the old Celtic languages. It is also called Gaelic. People speak Gaelic and English in Ireland.

The far west

Some of the most beautiful scenery in Europe is in Connacht (*Cúige Chonnacht*) on Ireland's west coast.

Cliffs stand high above the sea, and sandy beaches stretch along the shore. Inland, there are lakes and rivers full of salmon and trout. Dark peat bogs lie below blue hills. In summer, the peaceful green fields are full of wild flowers.

But some of the land is poor and farming can be hard here. Many people have moved away to England, Australia and the United States of America to find work and a better life.

County Galway is in south Connacht. Galway City is the main town on the west coast.

▼ The west coast and the Atlantic Ocean

▲ A *currach* race

Off the coast, the Aran islanders fish from open boats called coracles or *currachs*. They are still made from cloth covered in tar.

A holy mountain

Most people in Ireland are Christians, and belong to the Roman Catholic church.

Many Catholics visit the mountain Croagh Patrick in County Mayo.

Saint Patrick, who is the patron saint of Ireland, is said to have lived here about 1500 years ago.

An airport was built at the nearby town of Knock because so many visitors come here.

Poets and farmers

Sligo is a county of woods and limestone hills. The poet W B Yeats grew up here.

The River Shannon is the longest river in Ireland. It runs for 258 kilometres (161 miles). Sheep and cattle graze on the farmland in Roscommon.

▼ Peat drying in the sun

Oceans and mountains

The province of Munster (*Cúige Mumhan*) is in the southwest of Ireland. Many people come to visit its wild coasts. Here, the River Shannon reaches the sea. The highest point in Ireland is in Munster. It is called Carrauntoohill.

County Clare lies on the north bank of the Shannon estuary. There are caves and springs in the limestone of The Burren. Although it looks bare, more than 1000 different kinds of plant grow here, including rare orchids. The town of Lisdoonvarna is famous for its healing springs and its music festivals.

▲ A burial place, or dolmen, on The Burren, County Clare.

▲ Cork City

The southwest

The city of Limerick dates from Viking times. There are castles and abbeys in the green fields and hills nearby.

Cork City is the second largest in the Republic of Ireland. There are ferries to South Wales and France from Cork.

Just outside Cork City is Blarney Castle. Visitors come to the castle to 'kiss the Blarney stone'. This is supposed to give them the 'gift of the gab', which means the gift of talking their way out of anything!

In the far southwest lies the Dingle, once a haunt of smugglers. This area is warm enough for palm trees to grow. Killarney is set amongst beautiful lakes.

Glass and stone

Waterford, on the southern coast, is another city founded by the Vikings. Today, it is a large port. It is famous for its fine glass, or crystal.

Inland, in County Tipperary, is a hill called the Rock of Cashel. The Kings of Munster ruled here for more than 800 years, until the Vikings came.

▼ Cutting Waterford crystal glass

To the east

Most people in Ireland live on the east coast.

The province of Leinster (*Cúige Laighean*) has seaports, sandy beaches and holiday towns. Inland, there are forests, lakes and hills. Butter, milk and cheese comes from the farms of the Central Lowlands.

A Christian holy man, Saint Kevin, lived at Glendalough in County Wicklow more than 1400 years ago. Hundreds of years later, when the Vikings came, people hid in the tall tower at Glendalough.

▲ St Kevin's Church, Glendalough

▲ A ferry at Dún Laoghaire

Along the Irish Sea shore

There have been many battles on the east coast. The Vikings,

burial places. The Hill of Tara was the most important centre in the ancient Celtic world. The High Kings of Ireland were crowned here.

Cows and horses

Many towns in the Central Lowlands have grown from Norman forts. One of them is the busy market town of Athlone. Today, the fields are peaceful and full of cattle. There are bogs and lakes where many different kinds of

Dublin

Dublin (*Baile Átha Cliath*) is the capital city of the Irish Republic. It is on the banks of the River Liffey, which flows into Dublin Bay.

Almost a million people live in the Dublin area. The city is Ireland's centre of law, business and education. It is a friendly place, with markets, coffee and tea shops and many pubs.

Dublin is linked with the rest of the world by its airport. The national airline is Aer Lingus. There are also ferries to Wales, England and the Isle of Man. Railways connect Dublin with other cities in Ireland.

▼ The River Liffey, Dublin

▲ Trinity College Library

Around the city

The Vikings founded Dublin. The Viking Adventure centre shows what city life was like 1000 years ago.

The National Museum holds jewellery and other Irish treasures which are about 1200 years old.

Trinity College holds the wonderful Book of Kells, which is also 1200 years old.

Phoenix Park is the largest city park in Europe. Part of it contains a Zoological Garden.

Beside the Liffey

The River Liffey flows through the middle of Dublin. Near the river, there are fine buildings such as the Customs House and the Courts.

The main shopping areas are O'Connell Street, north of the river, and Grafton Street to the south. Grafton Street leads to St Stephen's Green, where there are ponds and trees.

Christ Church cathedral dates from AD1038, and St Patrick's cathedral from 1191.

▼ A statue of Molly Malone, the famous Dublin shellfish seller

North to Ulster

There are nine counties in the province of Ulster. Three of them are in the Irish Republic. County Donegal has hills, shining sea lakes, or loughs, and small cottages. The Glenveagh National Park lies in the northeast. Donegal is famous for its tweed cloth. Many people speak the Irish language in this area.

County Cavan is hilly, with a lake for every day of the year! People come here for fishing and boating holidays. The source of the River Shannon is in northwest Cavan.

County Monaghan has small market towns such as Carrickmacross, which is famous for its lace.

▼ Lough Neagh, Northern Ireland

Northern Ireland

The other six counties of Ulster make up Northern Ireland and are part of the United Kingdom.

Some people know Northern Ireland for its violent history. Less well known is the peace and beauty of its countryside.

Derry is a hilly county. Its county town is Derry, or 'Londonderry'. It is Northern Ireland's second largest city, after the capital, Belfast.

There are beautiful lakes, or loughs, and mountains in Fermanagh and Tyrone.

Armagh is a religious centre, with two cathedrals.

▲ Belfast city centre

The coasts of Antrim and Down are spectacular. The strange rocks called the Giant's Causeway are here.

Inland is Lough Neagh. This is the largest lake in the British Isles.

Belfast

Belfast (*Béal Feirste*) is the capital of Northern Ireland. It stands on the River Lagan.

Belfast is a busy city, with an airport and ferries to England, Scotland and the Isle of Man.

Queen's University in Belfast is a famous centre of learning in Northern Ireland.

▼ A nature reserve, County Down

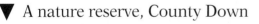

At work and at home

Farming is very important in Northern Ireland and in the south. Irish farms produce butter, milk, cheese, potatoes and meat. Fish farming and forestry, brewing and textiles are also important.

About a quarter of all workers work in factories, and nearly half work in hotels, banks and shops.

Ireland has some oil and gas. It also has large amounts of peat. Peat is burned in power stations to produce electricity. Peat is collected from bogs. Taking too much peat can cause damage to these wetlands.

▼ A farm in Northern Ireland

▲ Peat wagons at a power station

Irish homes

There are many kinds of houses in Ireland.

In the countryside there are big, old houses and castles. In the towns there are rows, or terraces, of small brick houses.

Some towns have fine old houses with big windows. The way these houses were built is called the Georgian style.

On the west coast, you can find small houses called crofts. They are built of stone with a thatched roof.

You can also find brightly painted, modern bungalows.

On the edge of some towns are parks for caravans. The Irish travelling people live here. They are famous for buying and selling horses.

Education and health

Education is free in Ireland. People can choose to pay to go to private schools. The Roman Catholic church runs some schools.

In Northern Ireland, there is a free national health service. There are also private hospitals. In the Republic, most people have free health care.

▼ A small house in the west of Ireland

Food and drink

Today, many people choose to eat lighter, healthier meals than in the past.

Some people start the day with a cooked breakfast of bacon, eggs and sausages. They may drink tea or coffee with their meals.

Lunch is between noon and about 2pm, and may be the main meal of the day, with meat or fish and vegetables. Supper, between 6 and 8 o'clock, might include sandwiches, cakes and cold meats or cheese.

▼ Fresh shellfish

▲ Bewley's famous café, in Dublin

Eating out

There are many good places where people go out to eat in Ireland. Some restaurants are in big houses in the countryside. Others are in the towns and cities. Some restaurants are small and may only serve one kind of food, such as shellfish.

Ireland is an island, so there are many different types of fish and shellfish to eat. Lobsters, prawns and oysters are famous. Some people like to eat a seaweed called dulse as well.

The best known dish in Ireland is Irish stew, which is lamb or mutton with onions, leeks and carrots. There is also 'colcannon' (boiled cabbage and potato pie) and 'champ' or 'stelk' (onions and cabbage).

Irish bakers make delicious cakes and breads, such as 'teabrack' which has currants in it.

Meeting friends

Dublin is famous for its cafés, where friends meet for tea or coffee and cakes.

The Irish pub is a centre for music and talk as well as a place to drink.

▼ Music and drinks in an Irish pub

Sports and pastimes

Sports are very popular in Ireland. Hurling is a fast game, played with a stick and a small leather ball. There are 15 players in each team. The team from Cork has often won the Irish hurling championship. Women play a type of hurling called *camogie*.

▼ A hurling match between Tipperary and Clare

▲ Northern Ireland and the Republic play each other at soccer

Gaelic football is like a mix of soccer, rugby and basketball! The players can catch, kick and punch the ball. They are not allowed to throw it. The goal has high posts and a net. Both women and men play this game.

A sporting nation

Soccer is the most popular sport in Ireland. The national team were heroes in the 1994 World Cup.

Rugby is also popular. The Irish team plays England, Wales, Scotland and France in the Five Nations competition.

Irish players have won success in athletics, boxing and cycling too. Michelle Smith won three gold medals for swimming at the 1996 Olympic Games.

Outdoors, people like to walk in the beautiful countryside, or to go fishing for salmon and trout.

A day out at the horse races is noisy and exciting. All kinds of different people go. The Laytown races take place on a sandy beach!

▼ Fishing in Ireland

Music and the arts

Irish music includes sad folk songs and wild dances. Fiddles, flutes, accordions, drums, tin whistles and the harp are very popular instruments. An Irish music festival is called a *fleadh*, or *fleá*.

Irish rock and folk musicians are widely known. Van Morrison and Sinead O'Connor are world famous. People of all ages love to dance, too.

Writers

There are poets and storytellers in Irish and in English. Some Irish stories are hundreds of years old. Storytellers used to tell the old tales from memory. In the Middle Ages, people began to write the stories down.

▼ Playing accordions and tin whistles

▲ A painting of W B Yeats

Oscar Wilde (1854-1900) wrote plays which are still popular.

The stories of James Joyce (1882-1941) and the poems of W B Yeats (1865-1939) are known all over the world.

Modern writers are also famous, such as the poet Seamus Heaney and Eilis Dillon, who writes children's stories.

Art and design

The ancient Celts made beautiful patterns of knots and animals. Christian craftworkers copied these patterns. They worked in metal and stone. They also decorated books, such as the Book of Kells.

People still make jewellery in Celtic patterns, and it is very popular.

▼ A page from the Book of Kells

Gaels and Vikings

People have lived in Ireland for about 10 000 years. In County Mayo, people have found fields where Stone Age farmers lived. At Newgrange there is a tomb made of huge stones carved with strange waves and zigzag patterns.

About 3500 years ago, Celtic people were living in central Europe. They started to spread out into other lands. Two groups of Celts came to live in the British Isles.

One group, the Britons, lived in Wales and Cornwall. The other group, the Gaels, lived in Ireland, Scotland and the Isle of Man.

The Celts brought with them the skill to make things in copper, bronze and gold.

▼ Stone Age remains in Cushendall, County Antrim

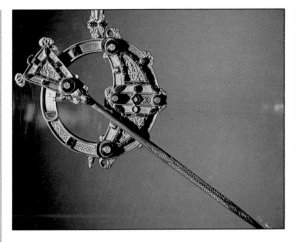

▲ The Tara Brooch is about 1200 years old.

The Gaels

The Romans conquered most of Europe, but they never ruled in Ireland. There were many local kings and queens. The High King ruled them all from Tara.

Around AD300, people invented a type of writing called 'ogham'. It was made up of scratches and lines which they carved on stones.

The stories of the ancient Celts are still told. They contain bravery and magic. Some of the characters include Queen Maeve of Connacht and the warrior Finn MacCool.

St Patrick was a Christian Celt. He came to Ireland in about AD432. While there were wars in Europe, Ireland was peaceful. People built monasteries and churches, and made beautiful works of art.

The Vikings

Between AD795 and 1000, the Vikings raided Ireland. They sailed their longships up the rivers, burned the towns and killed people. Later, they founded cities such as Dublin.

King Brian Boru fought the Vikings in 1014. He was killed, but the Vikings were defeated.

▼ The Ardagh cup, or Chalice, is about 1270 years old.

Rule from England

In 1066, England was conquered by French Normans. They took lands in Wales and Scotland, too. In 1168, the King of Leinster brought Normans to Ireland to help him fight other Irish kings. Soon, the head of the Roman Catholic church, the Pope, said that the Norman king of England, Henry II, was to rule all of Ireland.

By the end of the Middle Ages, the English ruled only a small part around Dublin. During the 1500s, England broke away from the Catholic church and became Protestant. England attacked Ireland again, and gave the Catholics' lands to people from England and Scotland.

▼ This drawing shows the death of an Irish king in battle. It was made in 1581.

▲ 'King Billy', William of Orange, at the Battle of the Boyne

Wars

There were many wars between the Irish and the English during the next 200 years. In 1690, the King of England, William, or 'King Billy' won the Battle of the Boyne.

In 1800, Ireland was made part of the United Kingdom. Irish Catholics could not vote in English elections. Their leader, Daniel O'Connell, helped them to win the right to vote in 1829.

Famine

About 150 years ago, a disease caused the potato crop to fail in Ireland. When poor people had no crops to eat or sell, they could not pay their rent. Many families were turned out of their homes. About a million people died of starvation.

Some people thought that the way to stop Irish people from suffering was for Ireland to rule itself. This was called home rule. One group thought force was the best way to get home rule. Another group tried to get the English parliament to agree to Irish home rule.

▼ When poor people were turned out of their homes, their houses were burned.

Free Ireland

The United Kingdom did agree to home rule, but in 1914 the First World War broke out, and Ireland was ignored. At Easter, 1916, Patrick Pearse and James Connolly led other rebels in Dublin against the British. They were defeated. The British arrested many rebels, and killed 17 men by firing squad.

Many Irish people supported the rebels. After the First World War ended in 1918, the Irish Republican Army (IRA) led uprisings around the country. The British sent a special force, the 'Black and Tans' to Ireland. There were many dreadful killings.

▼ The Easter Rising, Dublin, 1916

A new Republic

In 1922, Britain agreed to a new Irish Free State. Except for six of the counties of Ulster, Ireland would have some independence. Some Irish leaders wanted the whole of Ireland to be independent. Others thought that Britain would never agree to this. There was a civil war, and one of the leaders, Michael Collins, was killed.

Later, in 1927, another leader, Éamon de Valera, became the first President of the Irish Free State. It changed its name to *Éire* in 1937, and became the Republic of Ireland in 1949.

▼ An army patrol in Northern Ireland, 1987

New troubles

In the late 1960s, Roman Catholics in Northern Ireland thought that they were treated unfairly. They marched through the streets. Fighting broke out, and Britain sent in troops.

Since then, there has been fighting, bombing and terrorism. Many people have been killed. In 1994 both sides agreed a ceasefire, but it was broken. Now people hope that peace talks will make some progress.

▼ Children in the Mourne Mountains

Fact file

Government

In the Irish Republic there is no queen or king. The President is the head of state.

The head of the government is the Prime Minister, or *Taoiseach*. There are two houses of Parliament, the *Dáil* and the Senate.

Northern Ireland is part of the United Kingdom. People can vote for MPs who represent them in the House of Commons in London.

Flags

The Republic's flag is green, white and orange. Northern Ireland has the Union flag of the UK and the Red Hand of Ulster.

National anthems

The Republic's song, or anthem, is the 'Song of the Soldiers', *Amhrán na bhFiann*. Northern Ireland shares *God Save the Queen* with the UK.

Money

The Irish pound, or *punt*, (£) is divided into 100 *pingin* or pence. Northern Ireland has the pound sterling (£), made up of 100 pence.

Religion

Almost all Christians in the Republic are Roman Catholics. In Northern Ireland just over a quarter are Catholics, and the rest are Protestants.

Holidays

Holidays include St Patrick's Day (17 March) and, in the north, the day when William of Orange won the Battle of the Boyne. This is the Protestant Orangemen's Day (12 July).

News and broadcasting

The *Irish Times* and the *Belfast Telegraph* are well known newspapers. Irish television channels include Network 2, RTE 1 and BBC Ulster.

Some famous people

St Patrick (cAD385-461) introduced Christianity to Ireland. He is Ireland's patron saint.

St Brigid (453-523) was a nun. She is Ireland's patroness saint.

Brian Boru (926-1014) was the king who defeated the Vikings.

Grace O'Malley (Gráinne Ni Mháille, b1530) was a pirate chief.

Daniel O'Connell (1775-1847) was a lawyer and politician.

Constance Markiewicz (1868-1927) fought for independence.

Éamon de Valera (1882-1975) was Ireland's first President.

Mary Peters (1939-) is a Northern Ireland athlete and Olympic gold medallist.

Mary Robinson (1944-) is the first woman President of Ireland.

Gerry Adams (1948-) is the leader of a republican party, *Sinn Féin*.

Some key events in history

3000BC: Stone Age burials.

500BC: Celtic Iron Age.

AD432: St Patrick arrived.

795: First Viking raid.

1169: Normans arrived.

1556: Protestant settlers arrived.

1690: The Battle of the Boyne.

1800: Union with UK.

1845: The great famine began.

1916: Easter Rising, Dublin.

1922: The Irish Free State, civil war.

1949: Republic of Ireland formed.

1969: Marches, new troubles in Northern Ireland.

1973: Republic and Northern Ireland joined the EEC, now called the EU – European Union.

1994: Ceasefire and peace talks in Northern Ireland.

1996: Breakdown of ceasefire. New talks in Northern Ireland.

Index